be nice. the end. be nice. the end. be nice. the end. be nice. the end. be nice. the end.

be nice. the end. be nice. the end. be nice. the end. be nice. the end. be n ice. the end.

the end. be nice. the end. be nice. the end. be nice. the end. be nice. the end. be

nice. the end. be nice. the e be nice. the end. be nice. the e

the end. be nice. the end. be nice. the end. be nice. the end. be

Wendy

nd. be nice. the end. be nice. th e end. be nice. the end. be nice. th

Roger

nice. the end. be nice. the en be nice. the end. be nice. the en

end. be nice. the end. be nice. the end. be nice. the end. be nice. the end. be ni

be nice. the end. be nice. the end. be nice. the end. be nice. the end. be nice. the

the end. be nice. the end. be nice. the end. be nice. the end. be nice. the end. b

be nice. the end. be nice. the end. be nice. the end. be nice. the end. be nice. th

nice. the end. be nice. the end. be nice. the end. be nice. the end. be nice. the en

ISBN-13: 978-1-63489-466-1
Library of Congress Catalog Control Number has been applied for.
Printed in Canada.
First printing: 2022

26 25 24 23 22   5 4 3 2 1

Cover and interior design by Wendy Kieffer Shragg

Wise Ink Creative Publishing
807 Broadway St. NE, Suite 46
Minneapolis, MN 55413
wiseink.com

www.meettheplaygroundkids.com

The characters portrayed in this publication are fictitious. No identification with actual persons (living or deceased) is intended or should be inferred . . . except for the sweet little faces of the author and the illustrator, who are very real, and love sharing this book's important messages with you!

Be Nice.
The End.

Simple Wisdom of the Playground Kids

written by Bryan Skavnak and illustrated by Wendy Kieffer Shragg

For my kids.

b.s.

_____

For Eden and Jack, who bring joy to my heart every day.

w.s.

The playground is the microcosm of the world. Many different kids, interacting, trying to get along, trying to find a place to belong. From picking teams in kickball to jumping off the swings to playing tag, kids have things to say. And we should listen.

Because how we see the world differs from how kids see it.

They make it simple. They make it innocent. They make it real.

And these simple moments can help.

The wisdom of the Playground Kids is meant to be shared with friends, family, and kids of all ages. Even us grown-up kids. You may see something in one of their sweet, innocent faces. They may speak to your inner child.

If we take the wisdom of the Playground Kids to heart, we can teach, guide, and empower the people around us to be kind, caring, compassionate, and inclusive.

Their innocence. Their bluntness. Their simple take on kindness.

For the Playground Kids, it's easy.

Be Nice. The End.

Inclusion

One of the best feelings in the world is being included. Give it to someone else too.

What if we didn't turn away, but welcomed?
What if we didn't compare, but congratulated?
What if we didn't drag down, but teamed up?
What if we just helped more, cheered more,
praised more, and encouraged more?
What if?

Be the kid who looks out for others.

Want to play?
You can sit with me.
Would you like to join us?
Want to be in our group?
Come hang out with us.
It doesn't matter how you say it.
Just include others.

Be aware of who's on the outside, then let them in.

Include the kid who doesn't have anyone.
Include the kid who sits alone.
Include the kid who struggles.
Include the kid who is quiet.
Include the kid who needs someone.
Include the kid who is too shy to ask.
Include the kid who wants to be included.

When it comes to kindness, generosity,
and inclusion, it's not just about you.
It's about how you can make other people feel.

Do you want to make someone's day?
Include them. That's it.

Empathy

Be the kid who tries to understand
how others might feel.

Let other people be happy.
Let other people have the freedom to make their own choices.
Even if we disagree with something,
it's not our job to drag them down,
make fun of them, or find fault in what they do.
Everyone is unique. Everyone matters.

Wherever you go, whoever you meet,
and whatever you choose to do . . .
begin with kindness.

When you see struggle, be the support.
When you see fear, be the calm.
When you see doubt, be the belief.
When you see confusion, be the clarity.
When you see pain, be the comfort.

Sometimes other people need help.
So help them.
It's that simple.

Kindness can come from anywhere
and can be given to anyone.

Sometimes it takes just one person, one idea,
one thought, one chance, one try . . .
To make a positive statement.
To take a positive stance.
To make a positive difference.

Think, "Who needs me today?"
Find someone you can help.

Acceptance

Every day we come across people
who look different from us,
think different from us,
and act different from us.
But different isn't bad.
It's an opportunity—
to make a new friend,
to learn a new skill,
or to gain a new perspective.
Be open, be accepting,
and seize the opportunity.

Be the kid who can find common ground.

Be patient with people.
Maybe they are struggling in some way you can't see.
Be that extra dose of positivity they may need.

Be the kid who remembers that other people are different, and that's good.

There are others who might tease you
or be mean to you.
It happens to everyone.
But remember, there are many more who love you,
care for you, accept you, and are happy for you
exactly the way you are.

If they apologize, forgive them.
If they don't, forgive them anyway.
Let things go, clear your head, and move forward.

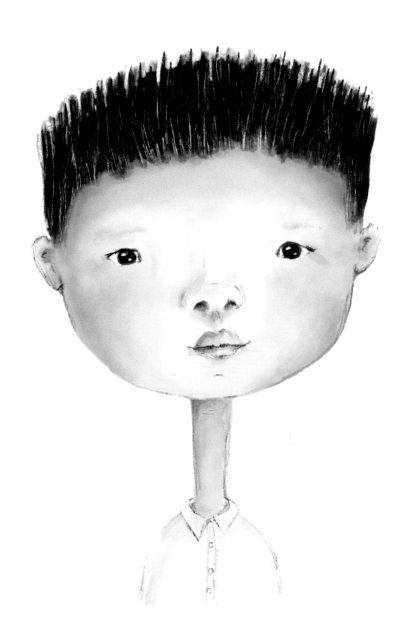

Let's listen.
Let's accept.
Let's use manners.
Let's stop making fun of differences,
and instead see them as opportunities.
But most importantly,
let's realize we all do better together.

Courage

If you see someone who finally built up the courage
to try something that scared them,
celebrate the attempt, not just the outcome.

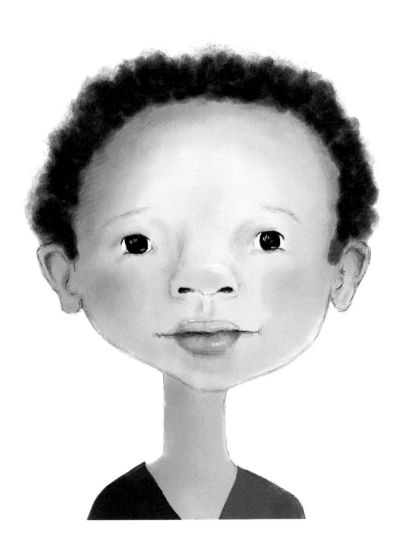

At some point you're going to lose,
and fail, and mess up, and be wrong.
That's okay.
Give congratulations after losses.
Learn lessons from failure.
Show grace in defeat.
And be proud of your character.

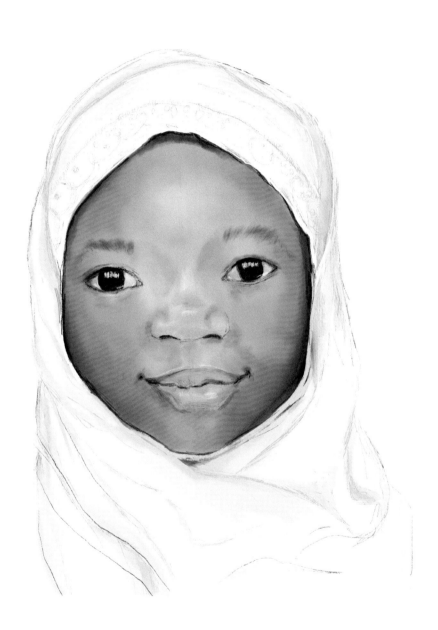

Sometimes we're faced with a choice.
Are we going to complain and blame?
Or are we going to work and get better?
Don't just work on what people see.
Work on attitude, mindset, positivity, and character too.

It's easy to think we're not good enough,
or smart enough, or strong enough.
But we are.
So if you see someone hurting, down, or discouraged,
give them a head nod, a high five, or a hug.
We have something to offer. We are valuable.
And we are good enough in our own special way.

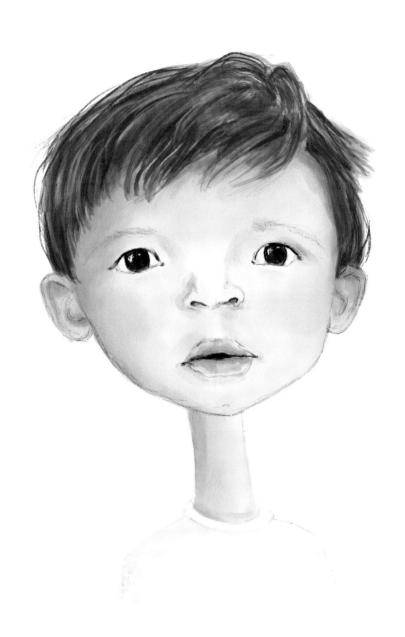

You can hurt people or you can help them.
You can make people feel bad or make them feel good.
You can pull people down or you can build them up.
It's a choice.
Good choices sometimes take courage.
Choose to do the right thing.

Be generous.
Be inclusive.
Not because you need to but because you can.
There are many things you don't need to do.
But if you can, have the courage to try.

Perseverance

When things seem tough and you don't think you can do it,
remember that you're not alone.
Everyone has their challenges.
Keep going.

Maybe you can't. But what if you can?

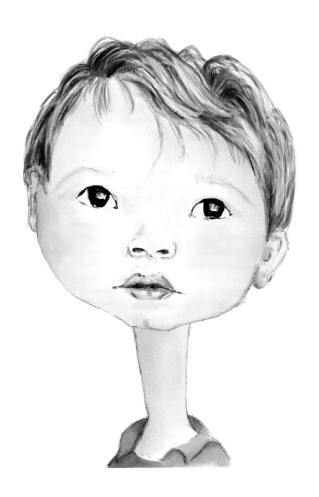

There are times we don't have the answer.
It's okay.
Make an attempt.
Try your best.

If you're confused or stuck
and don't know what to do,
be a good example,
be a good listener,
be a helper.

Be anything you want.
Just be something positive.

Keep being kind. Keep trying your best.
Keep making healthy choices.
Sometimes there are bumps along the way,
but keep going.

Perspective

When you think something bad might happen,
it might not.
The thing is, you never know.
Focus on the things you can control
and let go of the things you can't.

Start the day with gratefulness and end it with thankfulness.
Grateful that you get a chance to help someone,
and thankful for giving it your best.

Be the kid who knows that everyone
has something they're good at.

Life is about the people you're with,
the relationships you build,
the connections you make,
and the memories you create.

Try five things every day:
Give what you can.
Ask questions.
Listen more.
Laugh at yourself.
Play something fun.

Choose kind over mean.
Choose laughter over frowns.
Choose inclusion over exclusion.
Choose positivity over negativity.
Choose effort over laziness.
Choose compassion over selfishness.

Sometimes we're going to get angry or feel really mad.
But that's okay.
What matters is how we act on those feelings.

Sometimes you just need to let your
feelings happen.
Do an angry dance. Stomp your feet.
Scream. Cry. Take a deep breath.
You don't need to have the answers.
All feelings are allowed.

Be the kid who knows it's okay to ask for help when you need it.

See the good.
Lend a hand.
Try your best.
Be nice.
Negativity is easy,
but positive attitudes win.

You don't need to figure out
what you want to be when you grow up.
Just ask yourself . . .
who do you want to help?

Stop comparing yourself to others,
because you have your thing too.

Kindness

Make kindness a habit.

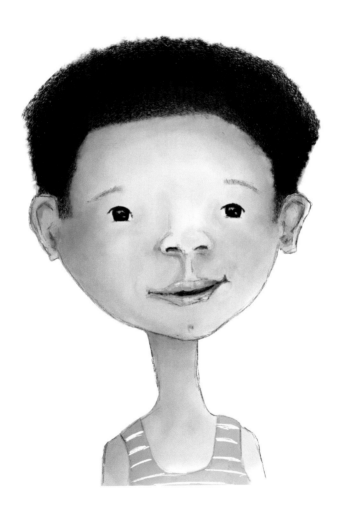

If you want to do something kind,
but you're not sure what . . .
Start small.
Say please. Say thank you.
Open the door for someone.
Say hi. Share. Pick up garbage. Listen.
Forgive someone. Use nice words.
Encourage someone. Give a compliment.

Be the kid who helps when nobody is looking.

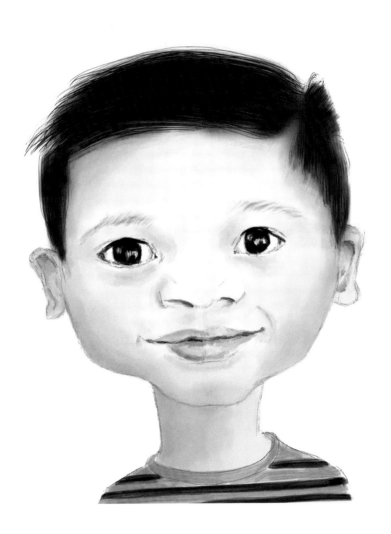

We can lead with kindness.

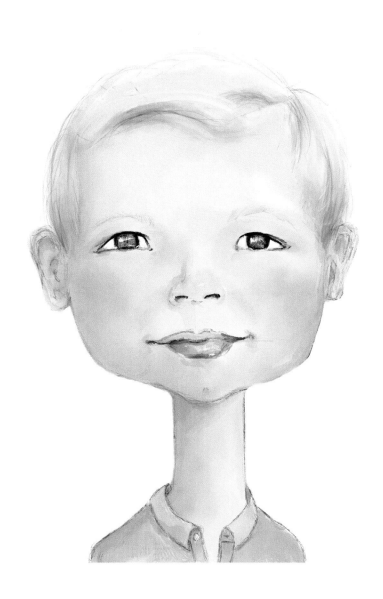

Take what you already have, what you already know,
what you're already good at . . .
and use it to help other people.

Every day . . .
do something nice for someone
and say something nice to someone.

Stand up for someone. It matters.

If you see someone you can help, lend a hand.

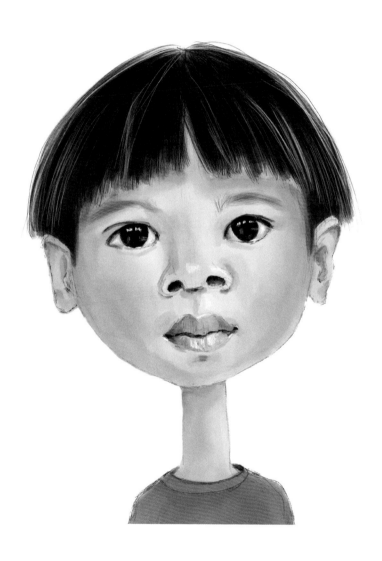

It's okay if you don't know everything right now.
But being kind, using your manners,
and doing the right thing is a good start.

It's time you understood your worth.
You are important.
You matter.
So let's show our best.
Let's stay positive.
And let's find the confidence to build each other up.

bethenicekid.com
thehappiestgolfer.com
@bethenicekid
bethenicekid

To book Bryan to speak at your event,
contact him at
bryan@bethenicekid.com

About the Author

I was a quiet kid.

I usually kept to myself. Sure, I had a few friends, but I wasn't the outgoing, talk-to-everyone type.

When my friends weren't around, I'd play Legos and build blanket forts. I'd play basketball by myself in the driveway, creating fictional teams with made-up players. (Aristotle Jenovosi was eight feet tall and Mitch Culpit never missed a three.)

At school, I tried my best and put in the effort to get good grades. Sure, there were kids smarter than me, but I was fine with that. Because there were also kids who were better at basketball than me. And who dressed better than me. And who had more friends than me. There was always someone better at something than me.

I was not Michael Jordan. I was not Michael Jackson. I was not Michael J. Fox. I wasn't even Anthony Michael Hall. (Man, there were a lot of famous Michaels in the late '80s.) I was Bryan Michael Skavnak. (Seriously, that's my middle name . . . see how I did that?) And Bryan Michael Skavnak was pretty good at something else . . .

I was good at being nice. Because I was taught that way.

I was taught to respect people and be kind to them. I was taught to use manners. I was taught to smile. I was taught to open doors and lend a hand and stick up for people.

Sure, I was picked on when I was younger. Because I wasn't cool. Or popular. Or the most outgoing. And yes, the saying may be true sometimes . . . nice guys finish last.

But I was okay with nice guys finishing last. Because I wasn't keeping score anyway. And I thought that way not because I didn't want to win or be good. No. It was because my parents also taught me not to compare myself to others.

One of my mom's favorite phrases is burned into my memory: "If Michael Bolton jumped off a bridge, would you too?" Okay, it wasn't Michael Bolton. But really, tons of famous Michaels . . . Michael Douglas, Michael Keaton. Back to the story . . .

I went through many answers to my mom's question, depending on my age and level of sarcasm.

"No, I wouldn't. Probably not. What's at the bottom? Do I have a parachute? Why Michael Bolton?"

But mom was right. We don't need to compare ourselves to other people or follow the crowd. Because we have our gift too. Each of us has something we're really good at.

I've taught golf to kids for twenty-three years. I've been around thousands and thousands of kids. Zero of those kids are on the PGA tour. Zero of those kids are on the LPGA tour. But a whole bunch of them are nice kids. They are kind and respectful and friendly.

They work hard. They take care of people around them. They do what's right. (And they stay in contact with me, which is the coolest.)

Sure, it would be awesome if someone went to play on the PGA Tour. But I teach kindness first. I teach being a nice kid first. Because at the heart of it all, and after your skills and accomplishments and victories fade away . . . you still have your character.

And character matters most.

wendyshragg.com
@wendyshragg_designs
Wendy Shragg Designs

To commission your own custom
Playground Kid, contact Wendy at
wendyshragg@gmail.com

About the Illustrator

For quite some time, I had felt an underlying tug that there was something I should be doing, a path I should be taking, but I just couldn't put my finger on it. I was looking so hard for what I felt was calling me that only by letting go of the looking and doing what I loved could I discover it was right there all along, waiting patiently for me.

The Playground Kids developed as part of #The100DayProject, a free global art project that encourages you to explore your creativity and share on Instagram each day for 100 days. In my first post, I stated that I was going to ". . . in some way get creative every day for 100 days. My thought is that I'll be using paint, but I'm going to treat myself kindly and allow the spirit to move me."

The creative piece of my life that had been my joy for so many years was urging me to play.

In the beginning, I used the challenge as a way to show people a glimpse into what I was working on in my studio—a way to chronicle my progress.

Things changed on day 34, when I introduced my first little friend. Day 35 brought another friend to the playground, followed by another on day 36. By day 37, I was hooked, and it was at this point that I began asking for help in naming these little sweethearts.

The response was amazing!

Day 100 was somewhat bittersweet.

There was the sense of accomplishment in committing to this project and successfully completing it, but there was also this longing for it to continue. These little loves were created from a place deep within my heart. Their innocence recalls childhood or the inner child that longs to hear inspiring words in a world that is moving so fast and has become challenging. Nothing can describe the depth of emotion I feel when I look into their eyes. They each carry a story within their little souls, and it has been my honor to bring them to life. The emotions they evoke in people have been heartwarming.

I'm an intuitively inspired artist who loves living a creative life. I have faith that art matters. It's one way we connect, heart to heart; to feel love, to feel understood, to know we are not alone and that someone else shares our story.

My hope is that you feel a connection with these little faces as well as the wisdom they share. It is my deepest joy to share my work with you.

This has been a journey of life and love and freedom of discovery. A learning curve that has proven that a practice is worth every moment invested. A journey that has opened doors and will continue to do so moving forward. I have grown in so many ways as a result . . . all from the decision to be kind to myself.

For more information on how to bring the Playground Kids to your school, office, or clinic, or to collaborate with Bryan and Wendy, contact them at:

meettheplaygroundkids.com
Instagram: @meettheplaygroundkids
Facebook: meettheplaygroundkids

Our Story

Sometimes collaboration can be easy.

Just like kindness.

But you may never know unless you just go for it.

In March of 2020, a mutual friend suggested to Wendy that she check out Bryan's Instagram feed. She loved what she saw. Bryan was sharing posts about the importance of things like kindness and acceptance and courage. Wendy instantly knew that these words could have come directly from the mouths of the Playground Kids she had created.

She was curious. How had he forged his path as a golf instructor to now reach people with these honest and simple words of wisdom? She reached out to Bryan. They had a delightful conversation where Bryan shared the story of how he developed "Be the Nice Kid."

Six months later, with a hopeful attitude, Wendy reached back out to Bryan with a simple question: "Want to write a book? My images, your words."

Without hesitation, he answered with a resounding "Yes!" Their collaboration began to share the innocence and thoughtfulness of the Playground Kids with the world. Kindness and goodness and inclusion come in all forms. They both felt they wanted to bring their unique perspectives together and create something special.

Throughout the next months, many meetings of the minds took place. They began to seamlessly fit together what they saw as timeless lessons for kids and adults. Wendy, with her beautiful images, and Bryan, with his thoughtful words, were a perfect match. An artistic endeavor with an important message.

Whether you're an adult, a child, or reconnecting with your inner child, this book will take you on a journey of discovery. It will remind you that you are unique and who you are is not only okay, but somebody to celebrate. The hope is that it becomes a staple in homes, schools, clinics, and anywhere else it's important to share and discuss the simple wisdom of the Playground Kids.

When it comes right down to it, we are all Playground Kids. And we can all be nice kids.

Playground Kids + Nice Kids = Be Nice. The End.

be nice. the end.

be nice. the end.

be nice. the end.